Mister Doctor

Mister Doctor

JANUSZ KORCZAK & THE ORPHANS OF THE WARSAW GHETTO

STORY BY **Irène Cohen-Janca**
ART BY **Maurizio A.C. Quarello**

Translated by Paula Ayer

annick press
toronto + berkeley + vancouver

"Doctor Korczak's been arrested!
Doctor Korczak's been arrested!"

"Doctor Korczak's been arrested!"

"They drove him far away from Warsaw

—to a labor camp in Lublin—and he died!"

"He was tortured and killed!"

"They took him into the woods and shot him!"

The shocking news spreads like wildfire.

Everyone thinks they know what happened. They're all telling different stories.

But we—we know none of it is true.

They couldn't have killed Doctor Korczak. It's impossible! He's too famous. He's a great doctor, a scholar, a writer. He has cared for the rich and powerful, he's given conferences all around the world, he's written books for grownups and children, and he even used to be on the radio. Everyone in Poland listened to the *Chats with the Old Doctor*.

But most important, Doctor Korczak—Mister Doctor, as we call him—is the one who protects us, the orphans and the poor children of Warsaw.

2

Goodbye Krochmalna Street

Yesterday, on the 29th of November, 1940, we had to leave the Orphans' Home, our big, beautiful white house at 92 Krochmalna Street in Warsaw.

We left behind our washerwoman and Peter Zalewski, the giant who took care of the orphanage. He always let us work with him in his carpentry shop in the basement. Sometimes, for fun, he would tweak our noses with his big hands, but we loved him.

The two of them watched us leave, their eyes red and Peter Zalewski's face swollen from the German soldiers' blows.

They wanted to follow us to our new home, but they weren't allowed to come to *the other side*.

When we left the Orphans' Home, I saw Mister Doctor look up one last time at the little attic on the top floor. That was his room, with the big oak desk, the narrow iron bed, and books covering every wall. That's where he slept, fed the passing sparrows, wrote books to teach adults how to love and respect children, and invented novels with heroes who are children, too, like King Matt the First and Kaytek the Wizard.

He didn't live alone up there:

a little mouse named Perspicacity lived under the wardrobe and paid him regular visits.

Yesterday, with lumps in our throats, but our heads held high and songs on our lips, we reached our new home, 33 Chlodna Street, on *the other side*.

Doctor Korczak refuses to be sad or resigned.

When the war started and the German army invaded Poland in September of 1939, when the bombs rained down on Warsaw and ripped the sky with red lightning, Mister Doctor spoke on the radio to lift Polish spirits. He ran through the rubble and flames to help the wounded, and even played the clown so people wouldn't lose heart. And when the Germans ordered us to leave our house on Krochmalna Street, Mister Doctor wanted our departure to be like the journey of a great theater troupe, not a sad eviction.

We wove through the streets like a circus parade. All 170 residents of the orphanage—Felix, Aaron with the weak lungs, Jakub with his one leg, Mendel, Chaïm the rascal, Moniek, Ania, Regina, and all the others—we marched proudly behind the green flag of King Matt the First as it fluttered in the wind.

Mister Doctor, Madam Stefa, and the teachers accompanied our long procession.

We carried lamps and blankets, flags and drawings, even plants and little cages with our pet birds and animals inside.

We had tucked our Memory Postcards in our pockets, the ones Mister Doctor gives us so we won't forget things that happen in our lives—our good deeds as well as our bad ones. There are so many different cards: there's the Flower Card, which you get for peeling a bag of potatoes, or the Winter Card, for rising early. There's even the Tiger Card, for getting in a fight. And there's the Forget-Me-Not Card, for those who leave the orphanage.

If I take good care of Mietek, I'll get the Helping Card.

When a new kid arrives at the orphanage, he's helped for three months by someone older. I'm the helper for Mietek, who came in September.

Carts followed us with mattresses, coal, and bags of potatoes.

The streets were filled with people, looking sad and worried, moving along with all their things piled in handcarts or baby carriages, or on their backs.

They, too, had been ordered by the Germans to go live on *the other side*.

Mietek, who was holding my hand, kept asking, "Simon, are we going far away?"

"No, keep walking. A sparrow could go this distance with a few flaps of its wings. Puss in Boots could do it in a single step."

All the kids at the orphanage know Puss in Boots. The Doctor loves telling us stories—Cinderella, Aladdin . . . but especially Puss in Boots. I think it's his favorite, maybe because that little cat with his white boots and feathered hat, always using his wits to do extraordinary things for his master, can give courage to those of us who are poor.

At the end of a story, we always yell, *Again! Again!*

We often ask for the same story two or three days in a row, and Mister Doctor never refuses. He doesn't get annoyed by our questions or treat us as if we're stupid. He understands as if he's forgotten nothing about being a child himself.

Mister Doctor didn't even get angry when Halinka, who is always sweet, refused to eat her bread crusts, though she knows we're not allowed to leave food on our plates. Instead, he was patient and tried to understand. Halinka ended up admitting that her grandmother had told her stories about witches living inside bread crusts.

When a little one asked him, "If I imagine a tree, does that mean I have a tiny tree growing inside my head?" Mister Doctor didn't laugh at him.

He says that children are poets and philosophers.

Maybe other children. But not me.

If I had a poet's words, could I have explained to little Mietek how *the other side*, where we were going, was so close and yet so far away?

It was the same country—Poland. The same city—Warsaw.

It was very near Krochmalna Street. And yet

As we entered, we had to show our papers, as if we were going through a border crossing. That was when a German soldier confiscated the last cart in our procession—the one that was full of potatoes.

Mister Doctor was angry but he couldn't get it back and we had to keep going, had to enter the country of *the other side*.

It's a tiny little country, just a few square kilometers. It's surrounded by very high walls built by the Germans, and guarded at each of its twenty-eight gates by soldiers.

Before, it was a Warsaw neighborhood like all the others, where everybody lived together.

Now, it's a prison-country, created by the Nazis

the other side, which
they called the ghetto, was
like a foreign country.

to keep in the Jews.

All the Jews—old people, adults, and children like us. A tiny
country for thousands of people who have no jobs, no furniture, no
bread or coal.

The washerwoman and Zalewski the Giant couldn't follow us to the
ghetto because they're not Jewish.

It was the afternoon after our move when the rumors of Mister Doctor's disappearance started to travel up and down the streets of the ghetto.

We had noticed his absence as soon as we woke up.

Madam Stefa had been left all by herself to set up the new house. She was Mister Doctor's second-in-command at the orphanage, and when he was away, she took his place.

She may look severe, with her broad face and her short hair, but she watches over us and takes care of us like the mother many of us have lost.

She sees and hears all. She enters a room so softly you don't even notice. She is big and strong but she glides, lightly, like a ship on the water.

This morning, as always, she was wearing her black dress with the white collar. The big wart at the side of her nose trembled very hard when she spoke. We older kids were spinning around her in circles, asking, "Where is Mister Doctor? Where is Mister Doctor?"

Madam Stefa didn't answer, and looked very worried.

It was the messenger who told us:

"Very early this morning, Doctor Korczak put on his tall leather military boots as usual, but he didn't wear his old gray shirt, like every other day. Instead, he put on his Polish officer's uniform, the one he served in during three wars, and then he left with a firm and determined stride."

"To go where?"

"To go to the Blank Palace, and get back the cart of potatoes the German soldiers stole yesterday."

We didn't ask any more questions.

We knew all about the Blank Palace, the big mansion where the Gestapo—the German police—had installed themselves.

Mister Doctor had gone to throw himself into the lion's den, but what fairy could rescue him, what sorcerer's spell could make him slip through the walls of that place of violence and fear?

Everyone trembled when they passed the Blank Palace.

The house where gunshots cracked and screams echoed, day and night.

The House of Tears

Our new house, at 33 Chlodna Street, is not as big or beautiful as the one on Krochmalna Street. The Orphans' Home was a real palace, with bright-tiled bathrooms, porcelain washstands, flush toilets, a study room, a playroom, and even central heating.

For those of us who had once lived with our families in the attics and mezzanines of old, dirty, wobbly houses, it was incredible to live in that vast and beautiful mansion, built for rich and important people.

Mister Doctor believes that children, even the poorest ones, are important people who deserve all that beauty.

But this is our new home, and it's time to settle in! Before, this house used to be a school, so during the day we'll use the classrooms, and at night they'll be transformed into dormitories.

Madam Stefa quickly organizes everything with the help of the teachers and us, the oldest ones. She runs from one spot to another, giving orders, but she isn't her usual self. Her face looks serious, and not even the little ones can manage to pull a smile from her.

Soon everyone will find their place, their things. But without Mister Doctor, nothing will be as it was before.

The Republic of Orphans is over.

Yes, we had a real Republic

at the Orphans' Home, which we, the orphans, ran ourselves. We had a Parliament made up of twenty Members who decided important things, and above all, a Court, so there would be justice and our problems would be taken seriously.

"How do you make a complaint?" Mietek asked me, soon after he arrived.

"You already want to make a complaint?"

"Well, no, I just want to know!"

"It's very simple. You just write down your name, what you're complaining about, and the name of the person you're accusing, child or adult."

"Even a grownup can be accused?"

"Of course! Even Mister Doctor himself has been accused and sentenced when he's broken our Code. The Court always seeks the truth. Our Code has a thousand Articles, one for each offence. The first are for small things, but then they get more and more serious. Article 900 says, *We have lost all hope of seeing the accused change*—but even then, the person is allowed to stay, as long as someone still has faith in him. The last one, Article 1000, says, *We send the accused away from the orphanage.*"

"Does that happen sometimes?"

"Well, Mister Doctor doesn't think all children are angels. Take Fula, who was always pushing smaller kids around, or Abraham Pieklo, who wouldn't stop shouting at the teachers. Those kids had to leave."

Mietek was quiet for a long time, then asked, "So Mister Doctor doesn't love all children?"

"That's not the point, Mietek. Mister Doctor says that we don't have to love everyone, but we always have to respect them. At the Orphans' Home, that's a law."

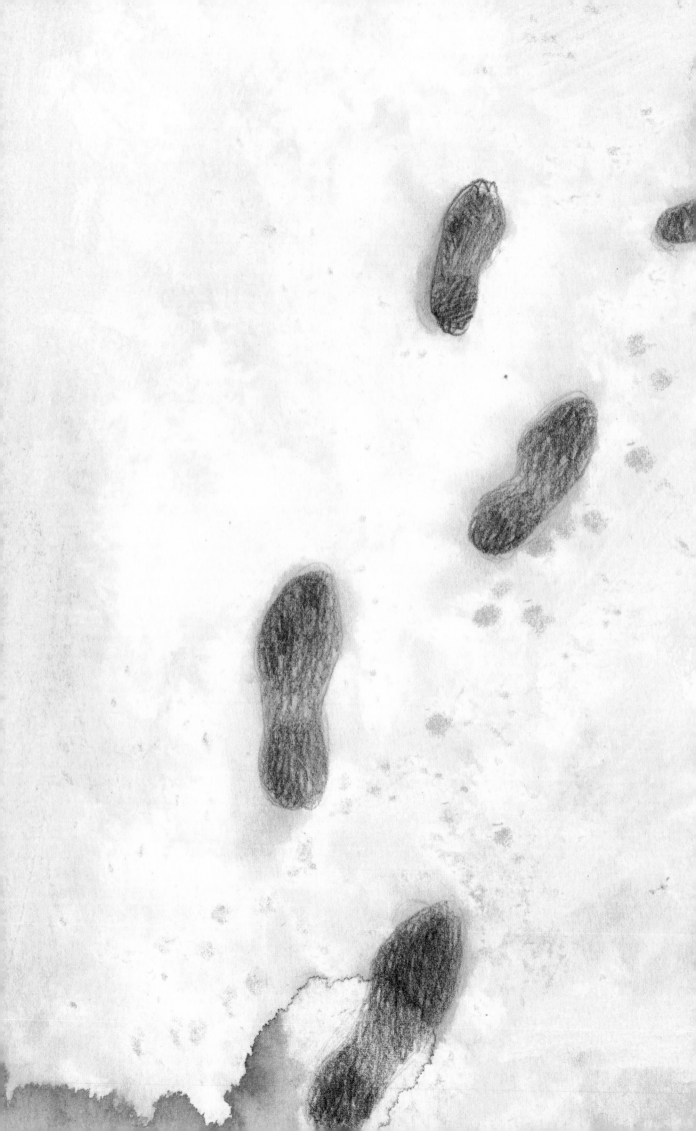

If Mister Doctor never comes back, all the wonderful things
he made for us at the orphanage will be gone. Our Court with a
thousand Articles. The glass case where we kept little objects we
found. The special letterbox for writing down our feelings when it
was hard to talk. The orphanage newspaper, *The Saturday Gazette*. The
notes he gave us to encourage us when we were down. The Memory
Postcards . . .

"Simon, why did Mister Doctor go to the Blank Palace when it's so
dangerous?" Mietek asks me now.

"Listen, Mietek, every day Mister Doctor goes up and down the streets
on his tired legs asking for money and food. That cart meant days and
days of work for him, and food for us. Those potatoes are precious—there's
almost nothing to buy in the ghetto."

"What if he doesn't come back?"

"He'll come back, Mietek, because we trust that he will—he's never let
us down."

I don't tell him that at the Blank Palace there is no court, or truth, or
justice.

Mister Doctor isn't dead!

Harry Kaliszer, who lived at the orphanage when he was a boy, managed to contact the Germans. He and some friends are going to try to pay a ransom for the Doctor's freedom.

Now we know what happened when Mister Doctor went to reclaim our cart of potatoes.

He thought that, with his Polish officer's uniform, his big boots, his scholar's glasses, and his little red beard, they would respect him.

At first the German officer was impressed. He didn't think that Mister Doctor, who spoke German very well, was Jewish.

But when he figured it out, he made fun of Mister Doctor's old, worn uniform and his authoritative tone. To the officer, he was just some old Jew who had the nerve to come and protest. And on top of that, he wasn't wearing the armband all Jews are required to wear.

So he insulted him, hit him, and threw him in a cell with some other prisoners.

How had they dared to hit Mister Doctor, who had never hit a child and had even fired a teacher for doing so?

I wish I could be as powerful as Samson in the Bible, who was blinded but brought a temple down on his enemies with his strength.

I wish I could be Aladdin, and rub my magic lamp to make the genie appear and free our old Doctor.

I wish I could avenge the father of all the orphans, of all the poor children.

But I'm only Simon. A Jewish orphan, prisoner of the Warsaw ghetto.

In our new house on Chlodna Street, life has settled into a
      routine.

            In the basement there's even a room for
      treating sick children. Madam Stefa doesn't
      want them to go to the ghetto hospital, where
      they could catch typhus or cholera. She doesn't have
      many medicines, but she knows how to treat patients
using simple things.

            We miss Mister Doctor, though.

            We miss how he would play pick-up sticks with us, or tell us tales
      and made-up stories, or put on concerts with the orphanage's little
orchestra. How he gave us courage.

      When we hurt somewhere, he rubs the spot, repeating *remedy, remedill,
remedy, remedill, nothing has happened, nothing will* . . . and the pain
disappears.

      At night, he walks between the beds and leans over to hear the breathing,
the coughs, the sighs. He can sense who is sick, who is unhappy, who is
afraid.

      Sometimes he sits down on a bench and at once all the little children
press against him, crowding into his space. Then he says that he's an old
tree on which children perch like birds.

      Often when he speaks, he caresses our cheeks, or puts his hand on our
heads. The palms of his hands are very dry and soft.

      Even with a crowd of people around, Mister Doctor's blue and piercing
eyes will notice the child who's sad and standing apart. He'll go to him,
touch his head, and whisper a few simple but precious words in his ear, like
a big secret.

Mister Doctor has come back.

But he's changed, a lot. Mietek hardly recognized him. He's pale and thin, shriveled and wrinkled like an old apple. His eyes are lined with red and his breath is wheezy. His eyes are shining, no doubt with the joy of seeing us again, but also with fever.

He spent a month in Pawiak Prison. It's now December.

We all lined up to greet him and the girls had prepared a little welcome speech. Then he quickly left us to go to his room, promising, "On Saturday I'll tell you about my adventures."

The day he came back, Mister Doctor asked for the door leading to the street to stay closed, and for no light to filter into his room through the night.

But on Saturday all his friends came to see him, and we found our Mister Doctor again. We shouted questions at him:

"What was it like in prison?"

His expression turned mischievous.

"Marvelous! My cell was as beautiful as the palace of King Matt the First. I slept well, I exercised, and I ate like a horse!"

He made us laugh by telling us how the most dreadful prisoners welcomed him onto their piles of dirty straw and demanded stories, just like little children. What we loved the most was when Mister Doctor described how he trained those big, tough men to catch fleas.

But Mister Doctor didn't say anything about how the Germans hurt him at the Blank Palace and in the prison.

Now, when he goes out in the street, he takes a cane.

On his first days back, he wouldn't even go out alone.

Our house is still a little bit like the world of before, thanks to Mister Doctor. But the ghetto outside is more and more strange and wretched.

Every day, Jews arrive from all four corners of the country, and there's less and less space for them. The streets teem with people and there are beggars everywhere, people in tatters trying to sell old things. Entire families sit on the sidewalks without a roof over their heads, huddled together so they won't die of cold.

The sidewalks are strewn with bodies—sometimes children, babies. They're covered with sheets of newspaper and thrown into the mass grave.

You can hear musicians and opera singers who were famous before the war but now beg for a few small coins.

The post office doesn't bring the mail anymore, and the parcels of food that Mister Doctor used to receive from all over the world are now forbidden.

The ghetto is infested with rats, and some boys have become as expert as cats at hunting them. There are also smuggler boys who try to get out of the ghetto, crawling through sewers or holes in the wall to reach the other side, where the normal world still exists. They try to bring back a bit of food for their families.

We don't have much to eat anymore. The soup keeps getting thinner, and many of us are sick.

But Mister Doctor wants life to go on and for our home to echo again with music, singing, and the sounds of puppet shows. Our house is an island in the middle of a furious ocean. Mister Doctor says each of us must look after our *inner castle* on that island.

He encourages us to keep a diary, like he does.

We read ours to him and in exchange we can read his.

We share. That's how I learned the story of the canary.

Henryk Goldszmit had a canary that he loved very much. One morning, he found it dead at the bottom of its cage. He wrapped it in cotton, placed it in an empty chocolate box, and decided to bury it under the chestnut tree in his building's courtyard. He even made a tiny cross to place on the little grave. But the caretaker's son stopped him, saying, "You don't have the right—you're Jewish, and your canary is Jewish, too."

Little Henryk, who was only five years old, was very scared. He worried that he and his canary would end up in a dark place and that Jews were forbidden from paradise.

When he grew up, Henryk Goldszmit took the name Janusz Korczak to write his books. He chose the name of a hero from a novel who was an orphan, just like us.

I wish I could go back in time and break the nose of the caretaker's son.

In the ghetto, schools are not allowed, but we go to class in secret.

Mister Doctor invites people to come and talk to us about their work, their passions.

We keep learning. Many, like me, learn Hebrew. When the war is over, we'll go to the Promised Land.

Mister Doctor has been there twice already, and he dreams of building an orphanage in the hills of Galilee. He would like a little room for himself on a terraced roof, with glass walls so he won't miss a single sunset and can watch the stars at night.

Yesterday, a professor, Mr. Zylbergberg, came to the orphanage to talk to us about a great Polish poet named Peretz who had lived very near us in Krochmalna Street.

He read us one of his poems, "Brothers."

It became a song:

Light and dark and in between,
All the colors come together.
We are all sisters and brothers
From one father and one mother,
And God created all of us.
The whole world is our nation.
We are all sisters and brothers.

We sang it several times,
arms linked and swaying.

We loved this song so much that,
along with Mister Doctor, we decided
"Brothers" would be the anthem of our
orphanage from now on.

The Last Move

On the 26th of October, 1941, we moved again.

Chlodna Street wasn't part of the ghetto any longer. We had to leave.

The Germans keep taking away space and adding more people.

Our new house, at 16 Sienna Street, is even smaller.

How long will we be here?

Everyone is worn out with hunger, illness, and worry.

We hear such frightening things. People say there are trains that leave for terrible destinations.

Will we see the end of the war?

Will we go back to Krochmalna Street one day?

Will Mietek and the other young ones be able to play and live like children?

Will we become Polish again, like everyone else?

On Saturday mornings, we pretend to be interested in reading the orphanage newspaper, but it never tells us the only piece of news we want to know: what's going to happen to us?

Because of the hunger and the worry, we're starting to look like little old people.

The ghetto is a country that keeps shrinking and closing in. Anyone who crosses the border without authorization is condemned to death. We don't know anything about what's happening over there, on the other side of the wall, where the Polish live.

It's farther away than America.

It's May of 1942 and there's no trace of spring. It's a frozen country here.

There are so many dead bodies in the streets that people passing by don't even pay attention now. The whole world has forgotten us.

Even spring has forgotten the ghetto.

The trees don't blossom and the grass is dying.

The birds don't fly in the black sky of the ghetto.

Some of the kids wrote a letter asking to go play in Grzybowska Place, in the church gardens.

To Mister Vicar of Toussaint parish:

Reverend Father, we humbly request your benevolence for permission to pay a visit sometime to the garden adjacent to your church, preferably Saturday between 6:30 and 10:00 in the morning.

We could really use a bit of fresh air and some greenery.

We are cramped in our place, and we're suffocating. We would like to get to know nature better.

We promise not to damage anything.

We would be very grateful to you for not turning down our request.

Zygmus, Semi, Abrasha, Hanna, and Aaron

That reminded me of the wonderful days of Camp Little Rose and our last summer there, in 1940.

Mietek has never been there, so I tell him about how we discovered nature, animals, and life in the country.

"Why," Mietek asks, "was the summer camp called Little Rose?"

"The people who gave the land to Mister Doctor had a little girl who died. Her name was Rose, so that's what we named the camp."

"What did you do there?"

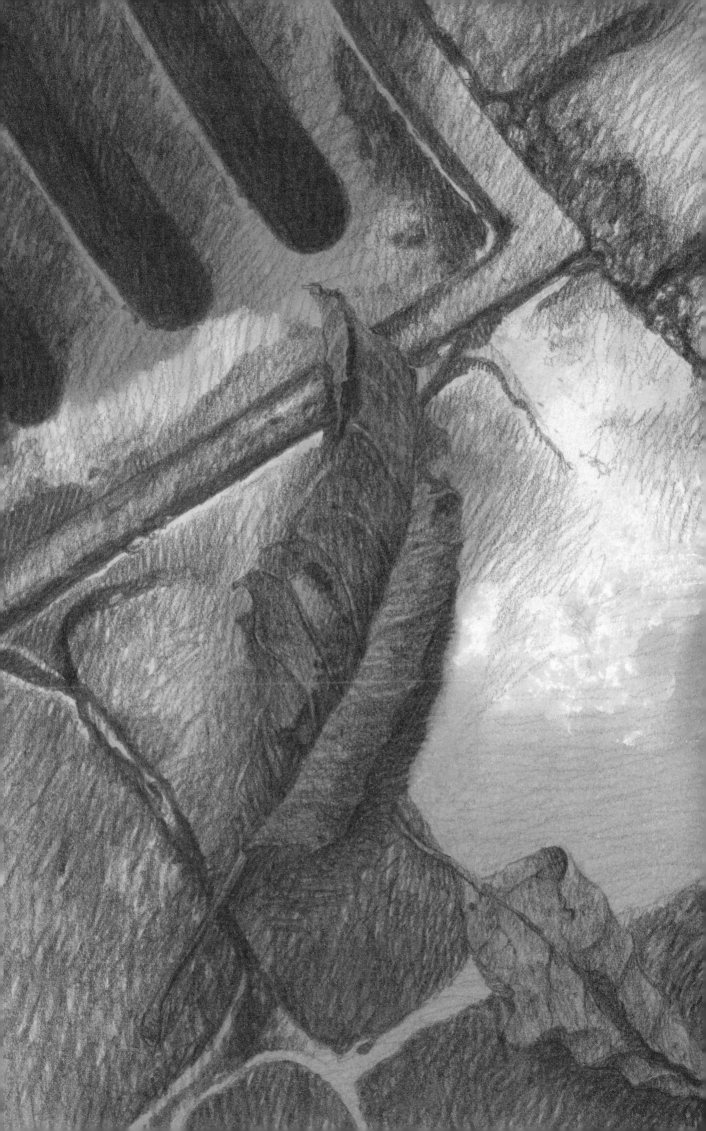

"We went for four long weeks in the summer, and we discovered a world that we never could have imagined in our old Warsaw streets, in our gloomy, closed-up courtyards.

"For the first time, we saw a forest and a sunset.

"There were birch trees with squirrels living in the branches. We learned how potatoes grow, what a plow is, how to milk a cow, and the most amazing thing of all—a newborn foal.

"Mister Doctor said that those four weeks should be like *one long day of happiness and play.*

"We showed our bravery at that camp! People who don't like Jews say we're cowards, but no way! We jumped in the cold river water just like the other children! We hit the water and splashed, just like them!"

In Mietek's thin, pale face, his large, dark-ringed eyes reflect the light and the clear sky of Little Rose.

I stop telling the story because all of a sudden a thought comes to me: Mietek will never see a foal lift itself up on its fragile legs or know the coolness of river water or the joy of squirrels leaping through the branches.

The Germans don't want Jewish children to grow up.

Everyone at the orphanage loves Abrasha, the violin player.

He was the one chosen for the lead role of Amal in the play we're going to put on today—the 18th of July, 1942, at 4:30, on the first floor in the main room.

The play is called *The Post Office* and it was written by an Indian writer named Tagore. We've put on our best costumes and the room is full.

It's the story of a sick boy—Amal—who is confined to his bed. People pass in front of his window: the watchman, a young flower girl, an old man, the dairyman. Children play and the flowers give off their perfume. Amal's love for all these beautiful things is immense and he wins the heart of everyone he meets. But he misses his freedom. He wants to run far away, toward the mountains, toward the river, to taste the sun's rays, hear the birds singing. He wants to leave this room, as sad and dark as the ghetto.

But the headman of the village tells him that soon the king will come to his bedside.

The king's doctor arrives, opens the windows wide, and lets in the night breeze. Amal feels no more pain and he falls asleep, softly.

He wakes up when the king calls to him and asks Amal to follow him.

We encircle Amal, forming a rainbow. His words enter us, bringing sweetness and calm.

When the play is over, a great silence descends.

In the darkness of our young hearts, we know who the king is.

He will come and deliver Amal.

He is the angel of death.

At the end, when the applause bursts out, Mister Doctor hangs his head.

It was very warm on the 5th of August, 1942.

It was still early in the morning when shouts and whistle blasts suddenly rang through the orphanage on Sienna Street.

The Germans had arrived by surprise.

In fifteen minutes all the residents were outside, assembled to go to the square from which the trains departed.

The procession of orphans moved forward. The oldest children carried the flag of King Matt the First, each in turn—Zygmus, Semi, Hanna, Aaron, Simon.

Behind them came Eva, Mendel, Hella, Jakub, Mietek, and all the rest ...

There were 192 children and 10 adults.

Old Doctor Korczak led the march, head held high, looking into the distance, a child on each hand. Another group, led by Stefa, followed.

Thousands of children came from other institutions, entire families joining them, dirty and sunburnt, filling the large square with crying and shouting.

They say a messenger came with a letter offering Doctor Korczak his freedom, but he refused to abandon the children.

The trains took them all away to the Treblinka camp, north of Warsaw.

It was their last journey.

Everything was taken from us, and in the depths of our hearts we knew we would never grow up.

But our anthem was called "Brothers."

We were murdered and given no graves, like the canary that little Henryk Goldszmit couldn't bury.

We were saplings ripped violently from the earth.

We never became trees or bore the fruits we should have borne.

But in watching us live, in loving us, in treating us with respect and admiration, Old Doctor Korczak championed the cause of children.

The Rights of the Child, now recognized the world over, are the promises we couldn't keep, the fruits we did not live to bear.

About Janusz Korczak

The real Mister Doctor was born in Warsaw, Poland, in 1878, and named Henryk Goldszmit (*Hen-rick Gold-schmeet*). He was Jewish, as were one in seven Warsaw residents at that time, and his father was a well-known lawyer. He became known as Janusz Korczak when he entered a writing contest as a young man, adopting his pen name—pronounced *Yah-noosh Kor-chock*—from the hero of a Polish children's book.

Korczak studied medicine and became a doctor at the children's hospital in Warsaw. He also served as a military doctor in three conflicts, including the First World War. Though he could have had a successful career as a physician, he gave it up to work with some of the most helpless members of society: orphans. In 1911 he became director of an orphanage for Jewish children at 92 Krochmalna Street in Warsaw, with Stefania Wilczyńska (Madam Stefa) as his closest associate.

At a time when children were often seen as incomplete beings who needed molding by adults, Doctor Korczak had revolutionary ideas. He believed children had the right to be respected, to be taken seriously, to make mistakes, and to be appreciated for who they were. He also thought that children had a right to justice, education, and a safe environment. And he believed they should be involved in running their own lives. At the orphanage, Korczak put those ideas into practice, forming a kind of children's republic run by and for the orphans, with its own parliament, court, and weekly newspaper.

During this time Korczak had also become a well-known writer. Many of his novels for children are about young people who must learn, through trial and error, to use their powers wisely. His most famous characters—the heroes of *King Matt the First*, a young prince who becomes ruler after his father dies, and *Kaytek the Wizard*, a boy with magic powers, much like Harry Potter— became as popular and beloved in Poland as Peter Pan or Lewis Carroll's Alice are to us.

Korczak wrote for parents and teachers as well, and his books, including *How to Love a Child*, forever changed the way adults viewed children. He was a popular radio personality, too, delighting 1930s listeners with his humor and wisdom as the "Old Doctor." However, after a few years his radio program was canceled because of a growing hostility toward Jews in Poland.

In 1939, the Second World War broke out, and the Nazis took over Poland. In 1940, Korczak and his orphans were forced to move to the Warsaw ghetto, where German soldiers were confining Jews, closing them off from the world outside. At its height, over 400,000 people lived in the ghetto—nearly a third of the population of Warsaw, in a space only 2 percent of the city's area. Food was scarce, and many people died from hunger and diseases.

By 1942 the Nazis had established extermination camps throughout Poland, where Jews and others who were viewed as enemies were sent into forced labor, or killed. In August of that year, German soldiers came to the orphanage at 16 Sienna Street, collected the nearly 200 children and 10 adults who lived there, including Doctor Korczak, and sent them on trains to the Treblinka extermination camp. They were never heard from again.

There's a famous story that when the orphans reached the Umschlagplatz—the square from which the trains departed—a German officer recognized Janusz Korczak as the author of one of his favorite children's books and offered to help him escape. Another story says the officer had orders to give Korczak special treatment because of his fame. Whatever really happened, Doctor Korczak refused to leave his orphans, and shared their tragic fate. As he had done throughout his life, he stayed true to his principles and didn't abandon those who needed him most.

Today, Janusz Korczak's story is well known. People still read his books, many of which have been translated into English and other languages. There are organizations around the world promoting his work and ideas. And his writings about children are considered an important influence on the Convention on the Rights of the Child, established by the United Nations in 1989—the first international, binding law to recognize children's rights.

Most of all, Janusz Korczak and the world he created for his orphans stand as an example of justice, kindness, and beauty in a world where those things seemed to have vanished—a shining light in one of history's darkest periods.

Further Reading and Resources

Children's Books About the Holocaust

Abells, Chana Byers. *The Children We Remember.* New York: Greenwillow, 2002.

Adler, David A. *Child of the Warsaw Ghetto.* New York: Holiday House, 2000.

———. *We Remember the Holocaust.* New York: Henry Holt, 1989.

Levine, Karen. *Hana's Suitcase.* Toronto: Second Story, 2002.

Rubin, Susan Goldman. *Fireflies in the Dark: The Story of Friedl Dicker-Brandeis and the Children of Terezin.* New York: Holiday House, 2000.

Children's Books by Janusz Korczak

Korczak, Janusz, translated by Antonia Lloyd-Jones. *Kaytek the Wizard.* Brooklyn, NY: Penlight Publications, 2012.

Korczak, Janusz, translated by Richard Lourie. *King Matt the First: A Novel.* Chapel Hill, NC: Algonquin Books, 2004.

About Janusz Korczak: Resources for Parents and Teachers

Holocaust Education and Archive Research Team. "Janusz Korczak." holocaustresearchproject.org/ghettos/korczak.html

Janusz Korczak Association. januszkorczak.ca

Korczak. Directed by Andrzej Wajda. Polish, with subtitles. New York: Kino Classics, 2012. First released 1990.

Lifton, Betty Jean. *The King of Children: The Life and Death of Janusz Korczak*, New York: St. Martin's Griffin, 1997. First published 1988.

Sanaeva, Galina, and Olga Medevedeva-Nathoo, eds. *Janusz Korczak: A Bibliography. English Sources 1939–2012.* Vancouver: K&O Harbour, 2012.

University of Minnesota Center for Holocaust & Genocide Studies. "Janusz Korczak's Biography." chgs.umn.edu/museum/responses/hergeth/bio.html

Related Links

UNICEF website. "Convention on the Rights of the Child." unicef.org/crc

© 2015 orecchio acerbo, Rome
Original Title: *L'Ultimo Viaggio*
Graphics: orecchio acerbo, www.orecchioacerbo.com
English text and afterword © 2015 Annick Press
First paperback edition, 2016

Copyedited by Melanie Little
Proofread by Catherine Marjoribanks

Cataloging in Publication
Cohen-Janca, Irène, 1954-
[Dernier voyage. English]
    Mister Doctor : Janusz Korczak & the orphans of the Warsaw Ghetto / story
by Irène Cohen-Janca ; art by Maurizio A.C. Quarello ; translated by Paula Ayer.

Translation of: Le dernier voyage.
Issued in print and electronic formats.
ISBN 978-1-55451-715-2 (bound).—ISBN 978-1-55451-861-6 (paperback).—
ISBN 978-1-55451-716-9 (html).—ISBN 978-1-55451-717-6 (pdf)

    1. Korczak, Janusz, 1878-1942—Juvenile fiction. 2. Jewish children in the
Holocaust—Poland—Warsaw—Juvenile fiction. 3. Holocaust, Jewish (1939-1945)—
Poland—Warsaw—Juvenile fiction. I. Quarello, Maurizio A. C., illustrator
II. Ayer, Paula, translator III. Title. IV. Title: Dernier voyage. English.

PZ7.C665Mi 2015   j843'.92   C2014-905947-7
                                           C2014-905948-5

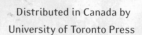

Distributed in Canada by
University of Toronto Press

Published in the U.S.A. by Annick Press (U.S.) Ltd.
Distributed in the U.S.A. by Publishers Group West

Printed in China

Visit us at: www.annickpress.com

Also available in e-book format.
Please visit www.annickpress.com/ebooks.html for more details.
Or scan